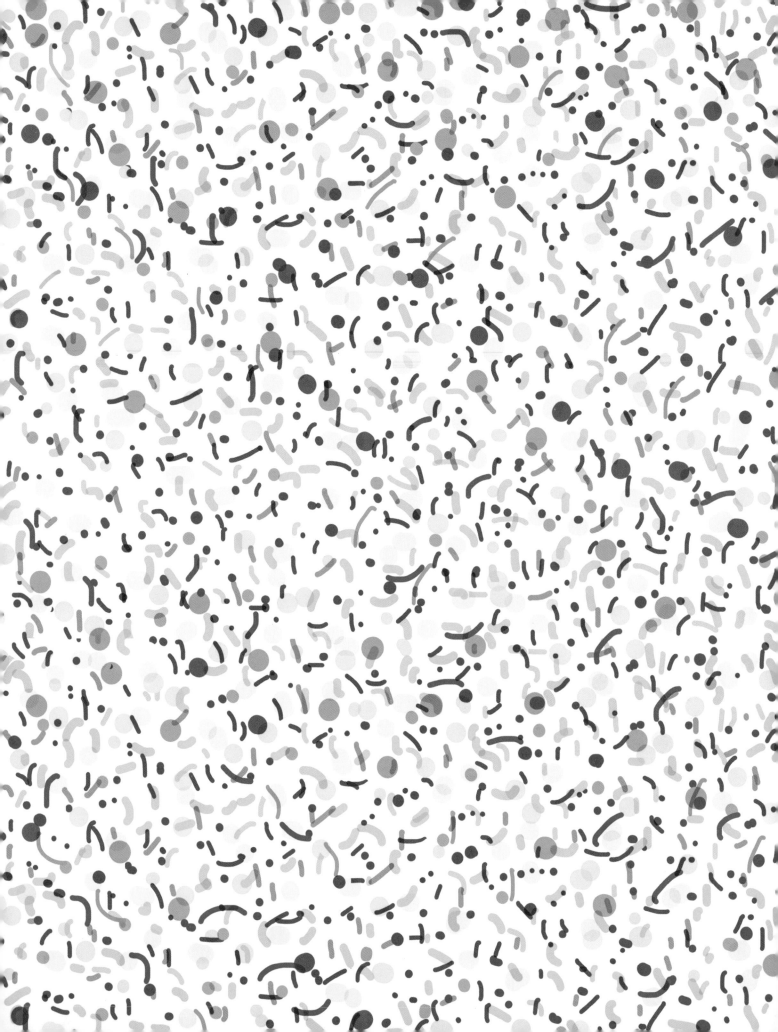

KIDS CAN BAKE

Recipes for budding bakers

Button
BOOKS

Illustrated by Esther Coombs

CONTENTS

BEFORE YOU BEGIN

Get ready to have lots of fun in the kitchen, learning basic baking skills and making delicious things for you, your family, and your friends to eat!

Baking isn't difficult, but there are a few golden rules you'll need to follow for baking success.

Before you start, read through the recipe first and check you've got all the ingredients and equipment you need, and you understand what you'll be doing. If you need to prepare any ingredients (such as melting, sifting, or beating), do this before you start to bake. And never start baking without the help of an adult!

Using an oven/ microwave oven

If you need to move any of the oven shelves, do this before turning it on. Cook food on the middle shelf of the oven, unless the recipe says otherwise. Don't open the oven door until the cooking time is up, unless you think something might be burning. Always wear oven gloves when taking anything out of an oven or a microwave oven.

STAYING SAFE

* Make sure there's an adult there to help you.

* Always wash your hands before you start baking, and when you've finished. Wash them after handling raw meat or fish, too.

* If you're wearing rings, take them off.

* Tie long hair back and wear an apron.

* Be very careful when using a sharp knife or a vegetable peeler.

* Never leave the kitchen when the burners are on.

* Use oven gloves when handling anything hot, and put hot dishes onto a trivet or heatproof mat.

* Turn pot handles to the side of the stove top to keep them safely out of the way.

* Be very careful when boiling things, especially syrup and sugar.

EQUIPMENT

You don't need loads of fancy equipment to make the recipes in this book, but here are some really useful things to have in your kitchen.

Pastry brush

Large metal spoon

Measuring jug

Measuring spoons

Kitchen scales

Pastry cutters

Large mixing bowl

Whisk

Palette knife

Sieve

Box grater

Oven gloves

Baking sheet

Cake pan

Citrus squeezer

Wooden spoon

Muffin pan

Wire rack

Rolling pin

Kitchen scissors

Sharp knife

BASIC TECHNIQUES

How to line a cake pan

Round

Cut a strip of paper long enough to go around the pan. Fold back 1in all the way along the strip and snip into it with scissors.

Press the strip around the inside of the pan, with the snipped tabs at the bottom. Put the pan on the paper and draw around the base.

Cut out the circle and use to line the base.

Square or rectangular

Place the pan on the paper and cut a square or rectangle that is 2in bigger than the pan.

Cut into each corner with scissors.

Press the paper into the pan, overlapping the corners so that it fits snugly.

How to crack an egg

Hold the egg in one hand, over a cup or bowl. Tap the middle of the egg with a knife to crack it.

Push your thumbs into the crack and pull apart.

Let the insides fall into the bowl. It's best to crack eggs into a separate cup or bowl before adding to your mixture in case bits of the shell fall in there too!

How to separate an egg

Place 2 bowls on the work surface. Hold the egg in one hand, over one of the bowls. Crack the egg. Push your thumbs into the crack and pull slightly apart, tipping the yolk into one half of the shell as you do.

Let the egg white fall into the bowl, then carefully tip the yolk into the other half of the shell and let the rest of the white fall into the bowl. Tip the yolk out into the other bowl. This is a bit tricky, so you might need to practice a few times!

How to beat an egg

Put your bowl on top of a damp cloth to stop it moving around. Beat the egg with a fork or whisk until it's frothy.

How to beat a mixture

Put your bowl on top of a damp cloth to stop it moving around. Use a wooden spoon to quickly stir the ingredients together until they are smooth and creamy.

How to rub in

Rub the butter into the flour using just your fingertips. Lift your hands above the bowl to let air into the mixture. Keep going until you have an even, crumbly mixture that looks like breadcrumbs.

How to sift flour

Put a sieve over a large bowl and spoon in the flour or confectioners' sugar. Lift the sieve slightly and shake it from side to side. You may need to use a spoon to rub any large bits through the sieve.

How to fold in

Use a metal spoon to gently mix the ingredients. Move the spoon around the edge of the bowl, then fold the mixture over into the center, and cut down through the middle. Repeat until everything is well mixed.

How to see if a mixture is soft enough

Lift a spoonful of mixture above the bowl and give it a gentle shake. If it drops easily off the spoon, the mixture is the right consistency, which means it isn't too runny or too thick. This is called dropping consistency.

How to knead dough

Sprinkle a little flour onto your work surface and place the dough in front of you. Using your right hand, push the dough away from you and over to the left in a diagonal line, and then bring it back to the middle. Then, do the same but use your left hand and push the dough over to the right. Keep doing this until it's smooth and stretchy (this takes about 5 to 10 minutes).

How to knock back dough

Punch down firmly with your fist to knock the air out of the dough.

How to roll out pastry or dough

Sprinkle a little flour onto your work surface and rolling pin. Press down with the rolling pin and roll across the top of the pastry, away from you. Turn the pastry and sprinkle more flour if needed. Keep rolling and turning until the pastry is the shape and thickness you need.

How to see if a cake is cooked

Insert a skewer into the center of the cake. If it comes out clean, it's cooked. If there's mixture on the skewer, put the cake back in the oven and bake for a few minutes before testing again.

SOFT PRETZELS

Ingredients

4 cups strong white bread
  flour
1 teaspoon fine salt
2 ¼ teaspoons dried yeast
2 tablespoons light brown
  sugar
1¼ cups warm milk
2 tablespoons (¼ stick)
  unsalted butter,
  melted and cooled

1 teaspoon vegetable oil
2 cups hot water
2 tablespoons baking soda
rock salt

MAKES 10

1 Sift the flour and salt into a large bowl, then add the yeast and sugar. Stir together with a wooden spoon. Make a hole in the middle of the flour.

2 In a jug, mix together the milk and butter. Pour into the middle of the flour and stir, bringing the flour in from the outside a little at a time. Mix to a soft dough.

3 Tip the dough out onto a lightly floured work surface and knead for 7 to 8 minutes until smooth (see page 7).

4 Wash and dry your bowl, then brush the inside with vegetable oil. Put the dough into the bowl and cover with plastic wrap or a clean dish towel. Put it in a warm place and leave to rise for about an hour or until doubled in size.

5 Mix together the hot water and baking soda in a wide, shallow bowl. (Be careful, it might fizz up a little.)

6 Knock back the dough (see page 7), then tip out onto a lightly floured work surface. Divide into 10 equal-sized pieces.

7 Take one piece of dough and shape it into a cigar shape. Place it on the work surface and gently roll it with your hands, starting in the middle and working your way out to the ends. Keep rolling until you have a long, thin rope about 22in long.

8 Make a circle with the dough, crossing the two ends at the top. Twist the ends around each other again. Bring the ends down and stick them to the bottom of the circle to make a pretzel shape. Repeat Steps 7 and 8 with the remaining pieces of dough.

9 Heat the oven to 400°F. Line 2 baking sheets with parchment paper.

10 Using tongs, dip each pretzel into the baking soda mixture, then place on a baking sheet. Sprinkle with a little rock salt.

11 Bake for 10 to 15 minutes until golden brown. Transfer to a wire rack to cool.

CORNBREAD

Ingredients

2 tablespoons (1/4 stick) butter, plus extra
for greasing
1 onion, finely sliced
1 ear sweet corn (or 3/4 cup fresh
corn kernels)
2 large eggs, beaten
1 cup coarse cornmeal
1/2 cup buttermilk
3 tablespoons all-purpose flour
1/2 teaspoon baking powder
salt and pepper
3/4 cup Cheddar cheese, grated (optional)

SERVES 6

Tips

* If you can't find buttermilk, add a squeeze
of lemon juice to 1/2 cup whole milk.

* Cut the bread into wedges and serve
with chilli, soup, or stew.

1 Put the butter in a frying pan and melt over a low heat. Add the onions and gently fry for 15 to 20 minutes until soft and golden.

2 With the flat end facing down, stand the corn on a chopping board. Hold the top and carefully run a small knife down each side to remove the kernels.

3 Add the sweetcorn kernels to the pan and cook for 5 minutes. Remove the pan from the heat and allow to cool.

4 Heat the oven to 400°F. Grease a 8in round cake pan and line it with parchment paper (see page 5).

5 In a large bowl, beat together the eggs, cornmeal, buttermilk, flour, baking powder, a little salt and pepper, and most of the cheese (if using) with a wooden spoon. Stir in the cooled onion mixture.

6 Pour the mixture into the pan. Bake in the oven for 35 minutes. After 10 minutes, sprinkle over the rest of the cheese and return to the oven.

7 Leave to cool in the pan for 10 minutes before transferring to a wire rack. Best served warm.

WHITE LOAF

Ingredients

4 cups strong white bread flour, plus extra
   for dusting

2¼ teaspoons dried yeast

1 teaspoon salt

1¼ cups warm water

2 tablespoons olive oil, plus extra for greasing

MAKES 1

1 Tip the flour, yeast, and salt into a large bowl and mix together with a wooden spoon.

2 Make a hole in the middle of the flour. Pour in the warm water and olive oil. Mix together to make a soft ball of dough.

3 Turn out onto a floured work surface and knead for 5 minutes (see page 7), sprinkling with a little more flour if it becomes too sticky.

Tip

Keep your bread fresh by storing at room temperature, wrapped in a paper or reusable cotton bag. Or slice and freeze for up to a month.

4 Grease a 2lb loaf pan with a little oil. Place the dough into the pan and spread out evenly. Cover loosely with a large plastic food bag or plastic wrap. Put in a warm place and leave to rise for about an hour or until the dough fills the pan.

5 Heat the oven to 400°F. Make several long cuts across the top of the bread with a sharp knife.

6 Bake for 30 to 35 minutes until golden. Turn out onto a wire rack. Tap the base of the loaf to check that it is cooked. It should sound hollow. Leave to cool.

FOCACCIA

Ingredients

4 cups strong white bread flour, plus extra for dusting
1 teaspoon salt
2 1/4 teaspoons dried yeast
4 tablespoons olive oil, plus extra for greasing
1 to 1 1/4 cups warm water

FOR THE TOPPING:
2 tablespoons olive oil
rosemary sprig, leaves picked

SERVES 10

OTHER TOPPING IDEAS
* thyme leaves
* sea salt
* chopped chilli
* olives
* halved cherry tomatoes

1 Brush a 12 x 8in baking sheet with olive oil, then dust with a little flour.

2 Sift the flour and salt into a large bowl. Stir in the dried yeast. Make a hole in the middle of the flour.

3 Pour the olive oil and 1 cup of the water into the middle. Gently mix with a wooden spoon to form a soft dough, adding a little more water if needed.

4 Dust the work surface with flour. Tip the dough out of the bowl and knead for 5 to 10 minutes until the dough is smooth and stretchy (see page 7).

5 Using a rolling pin or your hands, flatten the dough into a rectangle slightly smaller than the baking sheet. Roll the dough around a rolling pin to help you transfer it to the tray.

6 Cover with a damp dish towel and leave in a warm place for about an hour until the dough has doubled in size.

7 Heat the oven to 425°F. Push your thumb into the dough all over to make dimples. Drizzle with olive oil and scatter over the rosemary leaves.

8 Bake in the oven for 20 to 25 minutes until golden brown. Transfer to a wire rack to cool. Cut into squares and serve warm or cold.

PIZZA

Ingredients

3 cups strong white bread flour, plus extra
  for dusting
½ teaspoon salt
1 teaspoon superfine sugar
1 teaspoon dried yeast
¾ cup warm water
1 tablespoon olive oil, plus extra for oiling

FOR THE TOPPING:
1 x 14-ounce can chopped tomatoes
2 garlic cloves, minced
2 tablespoons tomato paste
1 tablespoon olive oil, plus extra for drizzling
handful basil leaves, torn
salt and pepper
pinch of superfine sugar (optional)
1 ball of mozzarella, torn into pieces
grated Parmesan cheese, for sprinkling

MAKES 2 LARGE OR 4 SMALL PIZZAS

EXTRA TOPPING IDEAS
* mushrooms * ham * pineapple
* olives * sweetcorn * tuna
* onions * anchovies * pepperoni
* grated Cheddar cheese

1 Sift the flour into a large bowl. Stir in the salt, sugar, and yeast. Make a hole in the middle and pour in the water and oil. Mix to form a soft dough.

2 Dust your hands and the work surface with flour. Tip the dough out of the bowl and knead for about 5 minutes until it's smooth and stretchy (see page 7).

3 Wash and dry your bowl. Rub the inside with a little oil. Place the dough in the bowl and cover with a clean dish towel. Leave in a warm place for an hour until the dough has doubled in size.

4 Put the tomatoes, garlic, tomato paste, and olive oil in a large saucepan. Place over a medium heat and bring to a gentle bubble. Simmer for 20 minutes until the sauce has thickened.

5 Remove from the heat and add half of the basil leaves. Season with salt and pepper. If the sauce tastes a little bitter, add the sugar. Leave to cool slightly.

6 Heat the oven to 475°F. Grease 2 baking sheets with oil. Knead the dough again for 30 seconds, then cut into 2 or 4 pieces.

7 Roll out each piece of dough into a thin circle about ¼in thick (see page 7). Place on the baking sheets.

8 Spread the tomato sauce thinly over the bases using the back of a spoon, but don't spread it to the edges—these will become the crusts.

9 Scatter the mozzarella and basil over your pizza bases. Top with a sprinkling of Parmesan and drizzle with olive oil. Bake for 12 to 15 minutes until golden and bubbling.

BEEF EMPANADAS

Ingredients

3 cups all-purpose flour, plus extra for dusting
1 teaspoon salt
1 teaspoon baking powder
$^1/_2$ cup (1 stick) cold unsalted butter, cut
    into cubes
1 large egg, beaten
$^2/_3$ to $^3/_4$ cup cold water

FOR THE FILLING:
1 tablespoon olive oil
1 onion, finely chopped
2 garlic cloves, minced
1 pound ground beef
1 tablespoon tomato paste
1 teaspoon ground cumin
1 teaspoon smoked paprika
salt and pepper

1 egg, beaten, for glazing

MAKES 15

OTHER FILLING IDEAS
* 2 $^1/_2$ cups grated mozzarella
* 1 cup ricotta cheese and
1 cup fresh or frozen berries.
For a sweet pastry, stir in
$^1/_2$ cup superfine sugar at the
end of Step 1.

1 Stir together the flour, salt, and baking powder in a large bowl. Add the butter and rub it in with your fingertips until the mixture looks like fine breadcrumbs (see page 6).

2 Using a knife, stir in the beaten egg and just enough water to form a soft dough. Bring the dough together into a ball, wrap in plastic wrap, and put in the refrigerator for an hour.

3 Heat the olive oil in a large frying pan over a low heat. Add the onion and garlic, and gently fry for about 10 minutes until softened.

4 Turn the heat up to medium and add the ground beef to the pan. Cook for about 5 minutes, stirring with a wooden spoon to break up the meat, until it is browned all over.

5 Stir in the tomato paste, ground cumin, and paprika. Season with a little salt and pepper. Remove from the heat and allow to cool.

6 Heat the oven to 400°F. Line 2 baking sheets with parchment paper.

7 Unwrap the chilled dough and place on a lightly floured work surface. Roll out to about ¼in thick. Cut out 15 disks using a 4½in round pastry cutter.

8 Put 2 tablespoons of filling in the middle of each pastry disk. Brush around the edge with beaten egg. Fold the pastry over to make a semicircle. Press the edges together with a fork to seal.

9 Place on the baking sheets and brush with beaten egg. Bake in the oven for 25 to 30 minutes until golden and crisp. Leave on the tray for 5 minutes before serving, or transfer to a wire rack to cool.

MINI VEGETABLE QUICHES

Ingredients

2 ½ cups all-purpose flour, plus extra
    for dusting
pinch of salt
¾ cup (1½ sticks) cold unsalted butter,
    cut into cubes, plus extra for oiling
4 to 5 tablespoons cold water

FOR THE FILLING:
1 tablespoon olive oil
1 carrot, peeled and finely chopped
1 red bell pepper, seeded and finely
    chopped
1 zucchini, finely chopped
2 large eggs
⅔ cup whole milk
salt and pepper
¾ cup Cheddar cheese, grated

MAKES 24

Tip

Store in an airtight container
in the refrigerator for up to 4 days, or
freeze for up to 3 months.

1 Sift the flour and salt into a large bowl. Add the butter and rub it in with your fingertips until the mixture looks like fine breadcrumbs (see page 6).

2 Using a knife, mix in the water, a little at a time, until the mixture starts to form a dough. Using your hands, bring the dough together into a ball.

3 Wrap the dough in plastic wrap and put in the refrigerator for 30 minutes.

4 Unwrap the dough, place on a lightly floured work surface and roll out to about ¼in thick. Cut out 24 disks using an 3in round pastry cutter.

5 Lightly oil two 12-cup muffin pans. Gently press the pastry disks into the cups. Prick the bases with a fork. Place the pans in the refrigerator to chill the pastry.

6 Heat the oil in a large saucepan over a medium heat. Fry the carrot, red bell pepper, and zucchini for 5 to 10 minutes until soft. Remove from the heat.

7 Heat the oven to 375°F. Beat the eggs and milk in a jug and season with a little salt and pepper.

8 Divide the vegetable mixture evenly between the pastry cases. Pour in the egg mixture until it comes halfway up the sides. Sprinkle with grated cheese.

9 Bake in the oven for 30 to 35 minutes until the filling is set and golden brown. Leave in the pans for a few minutes before serving, or transfer to a wire rack to cool.

CHICKEN PIE

Ingredients

1 tablespoon olive oil

4 skinless chicken breasts (about 1 pound), cut into chunks

1 carrot, finely chopped

1 large leek, thinly sliced into rings

2 tablespoons all-purpose flour

1¼ cups chicken stock

⅔ cup heavy cream

1 tablespoon wholegrain mustard (optional)

1 package ready-rolled puff pastry

salt and pepper

1 egg, beaten, for glazing

SERVES 6

1 Heat the olive oil in a large frying pan over a medium heat. Add the chicken and fry for about 4 minutes, turning occasionally, until lightly browned all over. Transfer to a bowl and put to one side.

2 Add the carrot and leek to the pan and fry for about 5 minutes until starting to soften.

3 Return the chicken to the pan. Sprinkle over the flour and mix well. Cook for 2 minutes, stirring occasionally.

4 Pour in the stock and season with a little salt and pepper. Bring to the boil, then turn down the heat until it is gently bubbling. Cook over a low heat for 5 minutes. Heat the oven to 400°F.

5 Remove the pan from the heat and stir in the cream and mustard (if using). Pour the mixture into a pie dish.

6 Carefully unroll the pastry and lay it over the dish. Trim the excess. Press the pastry onto the edge of the dish with a fork to seal.

7 Make a small hole in the top with a sharp knife so that the steam can escape. Brush with a little beaten egg to glaze. Bake in the oven for 30 minutes until the pastry is golden brown and the filling is piping hot.

JAM TARTS

Ingredients

1½ cups all-purpose flour, plus extra
   for dusting
½ cup (1 stick) butter, chilled and diced, plus
   extra for greasing
about 2 tablespoons cold water
4 to 8 tablespoons strawberry jelly or jam

MAKES 12

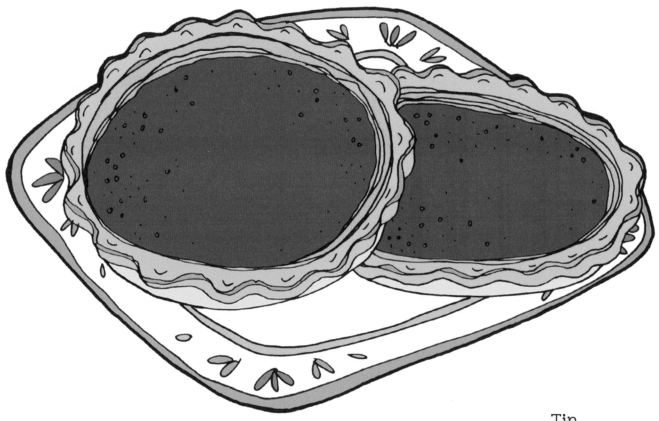

Tip

You can fill these tarts
with any type of jelly or
jam you like.

1 Put the flour and butter in a large bowl and rub them together with your fingertips until the mixture looks like fine breadcrumbs (see page 6).

2 Using a knife, stir in 1 tablespoon of cold water. Start to bring the dough together with your hands. If it's not coming together, add another tablespoon of water, or just enough to form a firm dough.

3 Wrap the dough in plastic wrap and chill in the refrigerator for 20 minutes.

4 Heat the oven to 400°F. Grease a 12-cup tart pan.

5 Unwrap the pastry and place on a lightly floured work surface. Roll out to about 1/8 in thick. Use a round pastry cutter to cut out disks of pastry big enough to line the cups in the pan.

6 Gently press the pastry circles into the pan. Spoon 1 to 2 teaspoons of jelly into each one.

7 Bake for 15 to 20 minutes until the pastry is light golden brown and the filling is starting to bubble. Leave in the pan for 5 minutes, then transfer to a wire rack. Be careful, the jelly will still be very hot.

APPLE PIE

Ingredients

6 Granny Smith apples, peeled, cored, and sliced

zest and juice of $1/2$ lemon

$2/3$ cup light brown sugar, plus extra for sprinkling

1 teaspoon ground cinnamon, mixed spice, or ground ginger (optional)

FOR THE PASTRY:

$2 3/4$ cups all-purpose flour

pinch of salt

$3/4$ cup ($1 1/2$ sticks) cold unsalted butter, cut into cubes

about 6 tablespoons cold water, plus extra for brushing

milk for glazing

SERVES 6 to 8

1 In a bowl, mix together the apples, sugar, lemon zest and juice, and cinnamon (if using). Put to one side.

2 Sift the flour and salt into a large bowl. Add the butter and rub it in with your fingertips until the mixture looks like fine breadcrumbs (see page 6).

3 Using a knife, stir in a tablespoon of water at a time, until the dough starts to come together. Use your hands to bring it into a ball. Wrap in plastic wrap and chill for 30 minutes.

4 Heat the oven to 425°F. Grease a deep 9in pie dish. Roll out two-thirds of the pastry and use it to line the base and sides of the dish.

5 Tip the filling into the pie dish. Brush a little water around the edge of the dish.

6 Roll out the last third of pastry to make a lid and place over the dish. Trim the excess. Press the pastry onto the edge of the dish with a fork to seal.

7 Use the pastry trimmings to make decorations for the top, if you like. Make a small slit in the top so the steam can escape, brush with a little milk, and sprinkle with sugar.

8 Bake in the oven for 20 minutes, then turn the oven temperature down to 350°F and bake for 30 minutes or until the pie is golden brown and bubbling.

VARIATIONS

Cherry pie

* Replace the apples with 5 cups of pitted cherries.
* Add 2½ tablespoons cornstarch in Step 1. Keep stirring until there aren't any floury patches left.

Peach pie

* Replace the apples with 6 peeled, sliced peaches.
* Add 2½ tablespoons cornstarch in Step 1. Keep stirring until there aren't any floury patches left.

COOKIES

Ingredients

½ cup (1 stick) unsalted
  butter, softened
¼ cup light brown sugar
¼ cup superfine sugar
1 teaspoon vanilla extract
1 egg
1¾ cups all-purpose flour
½ teaspoon baking powder
pinch of salt

MAKES 22 to 24

1 Put the butter and both sugars into a large bowl and beat together with an electric whisk or wooden spoon until the mixture is pale and creamy. Add the vanilla extract and the egg. Mix well.

2 Sift the flour into the bowl. Add the baking powder and a pinch of salt. Stir with a wooden spoon until well combined. Put the bowl in the refrigerator for 30 minutes.

3 Heat the oven to 375°F. Line 2 baking sheets with parchment paper. Use a teaspoon to place small balls of the mixture onto the trays. Space them well apart so they have room to spread. Flatten them a little with the back of the spoon.

4 Bake for about 10 minutes until they are brown at the edges and still slightly soft in the middle. They will look undercooked but will harden as they cool. Leave to cool for a couple of minutes, then transfer to a wire rack.

VARIATIONS

Rocky road cookies

* Replace ½ cup of flour with ¾ cup cocoa powder. Stir ¼ cup semisweet and ¼ cup white chocolate chips or chunks into the dough in Step 2.
* Push mini marshmallows into each cookie while still warm.

Oatmeal raisin cookies

* Replace 1 cup of the flour with 1¼ cups quick oats and gently stir into the dough in Step 2, along with ¾ cup raisins.

Chocolate chip cookies

* Gently stir in ¾ cup semisweet chocolate chips or chunks into the dough in Step 2.

Ginger cookies

* Sift in 2 teaspoons ground ginger in Step 2.

Chocolate chip & pretzel cookies

* Stir ½ cup semisweet chocolate chips or chunks and ¼ cup mini pretzels, broken in pieces, into the dough in Step 2.
* Decorate with pretzels at the end of Step 4.

Fudge cookies

* Gently stir ¾ cup fudge chunks into the dough in Step 2.

MACARONS

Ingredients

2 medium eggs
pinch of cream of tartar
$^3/_4$ cup confectioners' sugar, sifted
1$^1/_8$ cups ground almonds
$^1/_8$ cup superfine sugar
few drops of food coloring

FOR THE FILLING:
$^1/_2$ x quantity Buttercream or Cream
   Cheese frosting (see pages 62 to 63)

MAKES 12

Tip

If you want to use more than one food
coloring, divide the mixture into separate
bowls before you add the coloring in Step 3.

1 Grease and line 2 baking sheets with parchment paper.

2 Separate the eggs (see page 6). Put the egg whites in a large, clean bowl. (You won't be using the yolks in this recipe.)

3 Whisk the egg whites until they are stiff and stand up in peaks. Whisk in the cream of tartar, 2 tablespoons of the confectioners' sugar, and the food coloring.

4 Add the rest of the confectioners' sugar, one tablespoon at a time, whisking well after each spoonful.

5 Very gently, fold in the ground almonds and superfine sugar with a metal spoon.

6 Using 2 teaspoons, place 24 teaspoonfuls of mixture onto the sheets, leaving space between each one. Tap each sheet on the work surface 3 times to release any air bubbles. Leave to stand for 30 minutes. Heat the oven to 225°F.

7 Bake in the oven for 30 minutes. Leave to cool on the sheets.

8 While the macarons are cooling, make the filling (see pages 62 to 63). Using a palette knife, spread a little filling onto the flat side of a macaron and sandwich together with another. Fill the rest in the same way.

BRITISH SCONES

Ingredients

3 ½ cups self-rising flour, plus
    extra for dusting

½ teaspoon salt

2 teaspoons baking powder

¼ cup (½ stick) cold unsalted
    butter, cut into cubes, plus
    extra for greasing

2 tablespoons superfine sugar

1 cup milk, plus extra for glazing

TO SERVE:
Butter, jelly, and clotted cream

MAKES 10 to 12

Serving suggestions

British scones are best eaten freshly baked. Slice a scone in half,
then spread with butter and jelly or jam. Or, try with jelly and
cream. See if you prefer the jelly on top or the cream!

1 Mix together the flour, salt, and baking powder in a large bowl. Add the butter and rub it in with your fingertips until the mixture looks like fine breadcrumbs (see page 6). Stir in the sugar.

2 Make a hole in the middle and pour in the milk. Using a knife, gradually stir the mixture into the center to form a soft dough.

3 Heat the oven to 425°F. Grease 2 baking sheets.

4 Tip the dough out onto a lightly floured work surface. Using your hands or a rolling pin, gently flatten the dough to a thickness of about ¼in. Be very careful with the dough—scones can become tough if the dough is handled too much.

5 Use a 2½in fluted pastry cutter to cut out the scones. Push the cutter straight down into the dough and lift it out without twisting. Cut out as many as you can, then push the dough back together, flatten, and cut out some more.

6 Place the scones onto the baking sheets, leaving space around each one. Brush with a little milk to glaze.

7 Bake for 10 to 12 minutes until golden and risen. Transfer to a wire rack to cool.

CUPCAKES

Ingredients

½ cup (1 stick) butter, softened
⅔ cup superfine sugar
½ teaspoon vanilla extract
2 eggs, beaten
1 cup self-rising flour
2 to 3 tablespoons milk

FOR THE FROSTING:
1 x quantity Buttercream Frosting (see page 62)

MAKES 12

1 Heat the oven to 350°F. Line a 12-cup muffin pan with paper liners. In a large bowl, beat together the butter and sugar with a wooden spoon until pale and fluffy.

2 Beat in the vanilla extract and then the eggs, a little at a time.

3 Sift in the flour, then add 2 tablespoons of milk. Stir until smooth. Check that the mixture falls easily off the spoon (see page 7). Add a little more milk if you need to.

4 Use 2 teaspoons to divide the mixture evenly between the paper liners.

5 Bake for 15 to 20 minutes. Test with a skewer (see page 7). Leave in the pan for 5 minutes, then transfer to a wire rack to cool. Make the frosting (see page 62).

6 Add a nozzle to a piping bag, fill with frosting, and pipe swirls on the top of each cake. Or spoon a little onto each cake and smooth down with a knife.

VARIATIONS

Lemon cupcakes

* Replace the milk with 2 to 3 tablespoons lemon juice and add the zest of 1 lemon in Step 3.
* To decorate with a lemon twist, cut a thin slice of lemon. Make a cut from the outside edge to the middle. Holding the lemon slice either side of the cut, twist one side forward and the other side backward to make an 'S' shape.

Red velvet cupcakes

* Stir in 1 teaspoon red food coloring in Step 2.
* Replace ⅛ cup of the flour with ¼ cup cocoa powder and sift in ½ teaspoon baking powder in Step 3.
* Swap the Buttercream Frosting for Cream Cheese Frosting (see page 63).

Butterfly cakes

* When the cakes are cool, use a sharp knife to cut an upside-down, shallow cone shape out of the middle of each cake and cut in half.
* Fill the hole in the cake with frosting.
* Place the cut-out cake pieces on top, like wings.

MUFFINS

Ingredients

1 ²/₃ cups all-purpose flour, sifted
³/₄ cup superfine sugar
1 ¹/₂ teaspoons baking powder
¹/₂ teaspoon salt
¹/₂ cup milk
¹/₃ cup vegetable oil
1 large egg

MAKES 10 to 12

Tip

For fluffy, pillow-soft muffins, don't stir the mixture too much in Step 4. Don't worry if the batter isn't smooth—a few lumps are fine.

1 Heat the oven to 400°F. Line a 12-cup muffin pan with paper liners.

2 In a large bowl, mix together the flour, sugar, baking powder, and salt with a wooden spoon.

3 Pour the milk and vegetable oil into a jug. Break in the egg and whisk everything together until well mixed.

4 Pour the milk mixture into the dry ingredients and stir until just combined.

5 Use 2 teaspoons to divide the mixture between the liners.

6 Bake for 15 to 20 minutes until golden brown. Test with a skewer to make sure they are cooked through (see page 7). Transfer to a wire rack to cool.

VARIATIONS

Double chocolate muffins

* Replace ¼ cup of flour with ¼ cup cocoa powder in Step 2.
* Gently fold in ¾ cup chocolate chips or chunks at the end of Step 4.

Blueberry muffins

* Gently fold in 1 cup fresh or frozen blueberries at the end of Step 4.

Lemon & poppy seed muffins

* Mix in ½ tablespoon poppy seeds and the zest of 1 lemon in Step 2.
* Add the juice of 1 lemon in Step 3.

CAKE POPS

Ingredients

½ cup (1 stick) butter, softened
⅔ cup superfine sugar
½ teaspoon vanilla extract
2 eggs, beaten
1 cup self-rising flour, sifted
1 x quantity Buttercream
 Frosting (see page 62)

FOR THE TOPPING:
1¼ cups white chocolate
 sprinkles, to decorate

You'll also need 16 lollipop sticks.

MAKES 16

1 Heat the oven to 375°F. Grease a 8in round cake pan and line it with parchment paper (see page 5).

2 Beat the butter and sugar together in a large bowl with a wooden spoon or an electric whisk until pale and fluffy. Beat in the vanilla extract and the eggs, a little at a time. Fold in the flour with a metal spoon.

3 Pour the mixture into the pan and smooth the top. Bake for 30 to 35 minutes until golden brown. Test with a skewer to make sure it is cooked (see page 7). Turn out onto a wire rack and allow to cool completely.

4 Make the buttercream frosting (see page 62). Once the cake is cool, crumble it into the frosting in large chunks and stir together until well mixed.

5 Take small amounts of the cake mixture and roll it into balls about 1½ inches in diameter. Place on a plate lined with parchment paper. Push a lollipop stick into the center of each ball. Put the plate in the refrigerator for an hour to set.

VARIATION

6 Break up the white chocolate and place in a heatproof bowl. Microwave on high for 10 seconds, remove, and stir. Repeat until the chocolate is melted and smooth.

7 Dip the chilled cake pops into the melted chocolate. Hold over the bowl to allow any extra chocolate to drip off, then dip into the sprinkles. Stand upright in a mug and leave for an hour to set.

Alien cake pops

* Stir a drop of green food coloring into the melted chocolate at the end of Step 6.
* Once the cake pops are coated in chocolate, leave them to set for 20 minutes. Use black and white writing icing to draw an eye, mouth, and teeth. Leave to dry.

MADELEINES

Madeleines are small French sponge cakes that look like shells. They are baked in pans that have shell-shaped holes cut out of them. The holes are called cups or molds.

Ingredients

½ cup (1 stick) butter, melted and cooled,
  plus extra for greasing
2 eggs
½ cup superfine sugar
¾ cup all-purpose flour, sifted,
  plus extra for dusting
¾ teaspoon baking powder
zest and juice of ½ lemon

TO SERVE:
confectioners' sugar, sifted

MAKES 22 to 24

1 Using a pastry brush, grease a 12-cup madeleine pan with a little of the melted butter, making sure that the butter gets into all the grooves. Lightly dust with flour. Hold the pan upside down and shake to remove any excess flour.

2 Break the eggs into a large bowl. Add the sugar and whisk together until frothy.

3 Gently whisk in the melted butter, flour, baking powder, lemon zest, and juice. Leave the mixture to stand for 20 minutes. Heat the oven to 425°F.

Tip

Madeleines are best eaten on the day they are baked, but you can store them in an airtight container for up to 3 days.

4 Spoon half the mixture into the molds so that they are almost filled to the top. Bake for 8 to 10 minutes until pale golden, risen, and springy to the touch.

5 Carefully remove the cakes from the pan with a palette knife and place on a wire rack to cool. Once the pan is cool, repeat Steps 1 and 4, using up the rest of the mixture. To serve, dust with a little confectioners' sugar.

SWISS ROLL

Ingredients

4 large eggs

1/2 cup superfine sugar, plus extra for sprinkling

3/4 cup self-rising flour, sifted

4 tablespoons strawberry or raspberry jelly

1 Heat the oven to 425°F. Grease a 13 x 9in Swiss roll sheet and line it with parchment paper (see page 5).

2 Whisk the eggs and sugar together in a large clean bowl until pale, frothy, and thick. When you lift the whisk out of the bowl, it should leave a trail of mixture.

3 Gently fold in the flour with a metal spoon.

4 Pour the mixture into the pan. Gently tip the pan so that the mixture spreads evenly into the corners. Bake for 10 minutes until the sponge is golden, risen, and coming away from the edges of the pan.

5 While the cake is baking, place a piece of parchment paper slightly bigger than the pan onto the work surface. Sprinkle the paper with a little sugar.

6 As soon as the cake comes out of the oven, turn it out onto the sugared paper. Wearing oven gloves, peel off the parchment paper from the bottom of the cake and replace with a fresh sheet.

7 Starting at one of the shorter ends and using the bottom piece of paper to help you, fold over an inch of the cake to make the first roll. Continue to roll up the cake. Leave to cool.

8 When the cake is cool, unroll it and remove the paper. Spread the cake with jelly and roll it up again.

Tip

Rolling up the sponge as soon as it comes out of the oven stops it from cracking.

CARROT CAKE

Ingredients

1 cup self-rising flour

½ cup light brown sugar

1 teaspoon ground cinnamon (optional)

pinch of salt

2 eggs

¾ cup sunflower or vegetable oil, plus extra for greasing

2 medium carrots, peeled and grated

zest of ½ orange

⅛ cup sultanas (optional)

¼ cup walnuts or pecans, chopped, plus extra to decorate (optional)

FOR THE FROSTING:

1 x quantity Cream Cheese Frosting made with 1 teaspoon orange juice (see page 63)

1 Heat the oven to 350°F. Grease a 8in square cake pan and line it with parchment paper (see page 5).

2 Sift the flour, sugar, cinnamon (if using), and salt into a large bowl. Add the eggs and oil, and stir with a wooden spoon until well mixed.

3 Stir in the carrot, orange zest, sultanas, and nuts (if using).

4 Spoon the mixture into the pan. Smooth the top with the back of a spoon.

5 Bake for 25 to 30 minutes, then test with a skewer to make sure it is cooked through (see page 7). Leave to cool in the pan for a few minutes, then turn out onto a wire rack. Make the frosting (see page 63). Put the frosting in the refrigerator until ready to use.

6 Once the cake is completely cool, spread the frosting on top and decorate with nuts (if using). To serve, cut into squares or slices.

MARBLE CAKE

Ingredients

1 cup (2 sticks) butter, softened
1 1/8 cups superfine sugar
4 eggs, beaten
1 teaspoon vanilla extract
1 3/4 cups self-rising flour, sifted
3 tablespoons cocoa powder, sifted
2 to 3 tablespoons milk

Tip

Make a brightly colored marble cake by replacing the cocoa powder with
a few drops of food coloring in Step 5. You could also add a flavoring to
match. Try yellow food coloring and the zest of a lemon, or orange food
coloring and the zest of half an orange.

1 Heat the oven to 350°F. Grease a 8in round cake pan and line it with parchment paper (see page 5).

2 In a large bowl, beat together the butter and sugar with a wooden spoon or electric whisk until pale and fluffy.

3 Beat in the eggs a little at a time. Stir in the vanilla extract.

4 Fold in the flour using a large metal spoon.

5 Spoon half the mixture into a clean bowl. Fold in the cocoa powder until well mixed.

6 Stir a little of the milk into both bowls, adding a little more until the mixture falls easily off the spoon (see page 7).

7 Take a large spoonful of the plain mixture and place it into the cake pan, then place a spoonful of the chocolate mixture next to it.

8 Repeat with the remaining cake mixture, making sure that the bottom of the pan is evenly covered.

9 Bake for 45 to 55 minutes. Test with a skewer (see page 7). Allow to cool in the pan for a few minutes, then turn out onto a wire rack.

DEVIL'S FOOD CAKE

Ingredients

³/₄ cup cocoa powder, sifted
1 cup water, heated up
1³/₄ sticks butter, softened, plus extra
    for greasing
³/₄ cup superfine sugar
²/₃ cup light brown sugar
2 large eggs, beaten
2 cups all-purpose flour
2 level teaspoons baking powder

FOR THE FROSTING:
1 x quantity Chocolate Ganache
    (see page 62)

Tip
If you're baking this cake for Halloween, you
could decorate it with a pair of red horns made
from ready-to-roll fondant icing.

1 Grease two 8in cake pans and line with parchment paper (see page 5). Make the chocolate ganache (see page 62).

2 Heat the oven to 350°F. Stir together the cocoa powder and hot water in a bowl until smooth. Put to one side.

3 In a large bowl, beat together the butter and both sugars with a wooden spoon or electric whisk until pale and fluffy.

4 Beat in the eggs a little at a time until well mixed.

5 Sift the flour and baking powder onto a plate.

6 Using a large metal spoon, fold in about a third of the flour and a third of the cocoa mixture. Fold in another third of each. Fold in the last third of each.

7 Divide the mixture evenly between the pans and smooth the surface.

8 Bake for 30 to 35 minutes. Test with a skewer (see page 7). Leave to cool in the pans for 20 minutes, then turn out onto a wire rack to cool completely.

9 Sandwich the cakes together with a little ganache. Using a palette knife, spread the rest of the ganache over the top and sides to create a swirl pattern.

RAINBOW CAKE

Ingredients

1½ cups (3 sticks) butter, softened

1¾ cups superfine sugar

6 large eggs, beaten

4 teaspoons vanilla extract

2¾ cups self-rising flour, sifted

2 teaspoons baking powder

3 tablespoons milk

food coloring in red, orange, yellow, green, blue, and violet

FOR THE FROSTING:

3 x quantity Cream Cheese Frosting (see page 63)

sprinkles, to decorate

Tip

If you don't have 6 cake pans, bake the cakes in batches. Wash the pans after each use, then grease and line with fresh parchment paper before using again.

1 Beat the butter and sugar together in a bowl with a wooden spoon or electric whisk until pale and fluffy. Beat in the eggs a little at a time. Stir in the vanilla extract.

2 Fold in the flour and baking powder with a large metal spoon. Stir in the milk a little at a time until the mixture falls easily off the spoon (see page 7). You may not need all of the milk.

3 Heat the oven to 350°F. Grease six 8in cake pans and line them with parchment paper (see page 5).

4 Divide the mixture into six bowls and stir a drop of different food coloring into each one. Spoon each mixture into a cake pan.

5 Bake for 15 to 20 minutes. Test with a skewer (see page 7). Leave in the pans for a few minutes, then turn out onto a wire rack. Make the cream cheese frosting (see page 63).

6 When the cakes are cool, spread a little frosting on top of the violet cake and put the blue cake on top. Continue with the rest of the cakes, following the colors of the rainbow. Spread the rest of the frosting around the sides and on top. Decorate with sprinkles.

OATMEAL BARS

Ingredients

¹/₂ cup (1 stick) butter, plus extra
  for greasing
¹/₃ cup light brown sugar
2 tablespoons golden syrup
2 ³/₄ cups quick oats

MAKES 16

Tip

For vegan oatmeal bars,
replace the butter with
dairy-free spread.

1 Heat the oven to 400°F and lightly grease a 8in square baking pan.

2 Put the butter, sugar, and syrup in a saucepan. Melt gently over a low heat.

3 Take the saucepan off the heat and stir in the oats.

4 Press the mixture into the baking pan with the back of a metal spoon.

5 Bake for 15 to 20 minutes until golden brown and crisp. Leave to cool, then cut into squares.

Tip

To make gluten-free oatmeal bars, replace the oats with gluten-free oats.

VARIATIONS

Cranberry oat bars

* Replace the golden syrup with maple syrup.
* Stir in 1 cup dried cranberries, ½ cup sliced almonds, and 1 teaspoon ground cinnamon in Step 3.

Muesli bars

* Replace 2 cups of the oats with 2 cups of your favorite muesli.

Apricot & raisin oatmeal bars

* Stir in ⅔ cup chopped dried apricots and ¼ cup raisins in Step 3.

CHOCOLATE BROWNIES

Ingredients

1¼ cups semisweet chocolate, broken into pieces

⅔ cup (1⅓ sticks) unsalted butter, cut into cubes, plus extra for greasing

1¼ cups superfine sugar

3 large eggs

1 cup self-rising flour, sifted

pinch of salt

1 cup walnuts, chopped (optional)

MAKES 16

Tip

Brownies will keep for up to 4 days in an airtight container, or can be frozen for up to a month.

1 Put the chocolate and butter in a heatproof bowl. Microwave for 10 seconds at a time until melted. Or, place the bowl over, but not touching, a small saucepan of simmering water, stirring occasionally. Be careful, the mixture will get very hot.

2 Heat the oven to 350°F. Grease a 8in square baking pan and line it with parchment paper (see page 5).

3 Whisk the sugar and eggs together in a large bowl until well mixed and foamy.

4 Use a large metal spoon to fold the chocolate mixture into the eggs, then gently fold in the flour, salt, and walnuts (if using).

5 Pour the mixture into the pan and smooth the top. Bake for 20 to 25 minutes until just firm in the center. Brownies should be gooey in the middle, so try not to overbake them.

6 Leave to cool in the pan before cutting into squares.

VARIATIONS

Oreo brownies

* Replace the walnuts with 14 Oreo cookies, broken into quarters. Stir half into the mixture at the end of Step 4.
* Once the mixture is in the pan, scatter the rest of the cookies over the top, pushing them in slightly.

White chocolate blondies

* Replace the semisweet chocolate with white chocolate.
* Replace the walnuts with macadamia nuts or hazelnuts.

Peanut-butter swirl brownies

* Replace the walnuts with unsalted peanuts.
* Once the oven is hot, spoon 2 tablespoons smooth peanut butter into a heatproof bowl and place in the oven for 5 minutes.
* Once the mixture is in the pan, drizzle the peanut butter over the top. Using a skewer, make a swirl pattern.

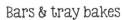

CARAMEL SHORTBREAD

Ingredients

2 cups all-purpose flour
$^{3}/_{4}$ cup superfine sugar
$^{3}/_{4}$ cup (1 $^{1}/_{2}$ sticks) cold
   butter, cut into chunks,
   plus extra for greasing

FOR THE CARAMEL:
$^{1}/_{2}$ cup (1 stick) butter
$^{1}/_{2}$ cup light brown sugar
1 x 14-ounce can sweetened
   condensed milk

FOR THE TOPPING:
1 $^{1}/_{4}$ cups milk chocolate,
   broken into pieces

MAKES 16

Tip
You could use
semisweet chocolate
instead of milk
chocolate for
the topping.

1 Heat the oven to 350°F. Grease a deep 8 to 8½in square baking pan. Line it with parchment paper (see page 5).

2 Put the flour and sugar into a large bowl and mix together with a wooden spoon.

3 Add the butter and rub together using your fingertips until the mixture looks like fine breadcrumbs (see page 6).

4 Using your hands, bring the dough together into a ball and knead a little until smooth.

5 Press the dough into the pan with your fingers or the back of a spoon. Prick all over with a fork. Bake in the oven for 20 minutes until pale golden brown. Leave to cool. (You can turn off the oven now.)

6 Put the butter, sugar, and condensed milk in a saucepan over a low heat. Stir with a wooden spoon until the sugar dissolves, then turn the heat up to medium. Keep stirring until the mixture comes to the boil, then lower the heat. Stir for 5 to 10 minutes until the caramel thickens slightly.

7 Carefully pour the caramel over the shortbread and leave to cool completely.

8 Put the chocolate in a heatproof bowl and place over, but not touching, a saucepan of gently bubbling water until melted. Or, melt in the microwave for 10 seconds at a time.

9 Carefully pour the melted chocolate over the cold caramel and leave to cool. Once completely set, dip a knife in hot water and cut into squares.

LEMON DRIZZLE CAKE

Ingredients

1 cup (2 sticks) butter, softened,
  plus extra for greasing
$1\frac{1}{8}$ cups superfine sugar
3 large eggs, beaten
$1\frac{3}{4}$ cups self-rising flour
2 level teaspoons baking powder
zest and juice of 1 lemon

FOR THE DRIZZLE:
$\frac{1}{2}$ cup granulated sugar
juice of 1 lemon

MAKES 20

Tip

To make a vegan version, leave out the eggs and replace
the butter with $\frac{1}{3}$ cup vegetable oil and $\frac{1}{2}$ cup cold water.
Use a whisk to mix everything together in Step 4.

1 Heat the oven to 350°F. Line a 12 x 8in baking pan with parchment paper so that it overlaps the edges slightly (see page 5).

2 Beat together the butter and sugar in a large bowl with a wooden spoon or electric whisk until pale and fluffy.

3 Beat in the eggs a little at a time.

4 Sift in the flour and baking powder. Add the lemon zest and juice. Fold in with a large metal spoon until well mixed.

5 Spoon the mixture into the pan and smooth the surface. Bake for 35 to 40 minutes until a skewer inserted into the center comes out clean (see page 7).

6 While the cake is in the oven, make the drizzle by mixing together the sugar and lemon juice in a small bowl.

7 Leave the cake to cool in the pan for 5 minutes. Holding the paper, lift the cake out of the pan and place on a wire rack.

8 Prick all over with a skewer or fork. Gently spoon over the drizzle, allowing it to soak in before adding any more.

9 Leave to cool, then cut into squares.

PROFITEROLES

Profiteroles are little buns made from choux pastry. Choux pastry is made in a saucepan, then baked in the oven.

Ingredients

¼ cup (½ stick) butter, cut into cubes, plus extra for greasing
⅔ cup water
½ cup all-purpose flour, sifted
2 eggs, beaten

FOR THE FILLING:
1¼ cups heavy cream

FOR THE TOPPING:
1 x quantity Chocolate Ganache (see page 62)

MAKES 16 to 18

Tips

* To stop the profiteroles from going soggy, fill them just before serving.

* Try filling the buns with ice cream!

1 Heat the oven to 425°F. Grease 2 baking sheets and line them with parchment paper (see page 5).

2 Put the butter and water in a saucepan. Place over a low heat to allow the butter to melt, then turn up the heat and bring to the boil.

3 Take the saucepan off the heat and add all of the flour in one go. Beat the mixture with a wooden spoon until it is smooth and comes away from the sides of the saucepan.

4 Leave to cool for 5 minutes. Add the beaten egg, a little at a time, beating with a wooden spoon to make a smooth, glossy, stiff mixture.

5 Using 2 teaspoons, place spoonfuls of mixture onto the baking sheets, leaving space around each one.

6 Bake for 18 to 20 minutes until puffed up and golden brown. Transfer to a wire rack. Using a knife, cut a small slit in the base of each bun to let out the steam.

7 Put the cream in a bowl and beat with an electric or hand whisk until just thick enough to hold its shape. Place in the refrigerator until ready to serve.

8 When you're ready to serve, make the chocolate ganache (see page 62). Fill a piping bag with the cream, make a small hole in each bun and pipe in the cream.

9 Pile the profiteroles onto a serving plate, drizzle with the warm chocolate ganache and serve straight away.

CAKE TOPPINGS

You can transform plain cakes into something really special with frosting. Here are a few to try...

CHOCOLATE GANACHE

Enough for an 8-inch cake or 16 profiteroles

Ingredients
½ cup heavy cream
¾ cup bittersweet chocolate,
  broken into pieces
⅛ cup (¼ stick) butter
1¾ tablespoons clear honey

1 Heat the cream in a saucepan over a medium heat. Just before it starts to boil, take the pan off the heat.

2 Add the chocolate, butter, and honey. Leave to melt for a few minutes, then stir until shiny and smooth. Drizzle over profiteroles straight away. Or pour into a bowl and allow to cool, then spread onto a cake.

BUTTERCREAM FROSTING

Enough for an 8-inch cake or 12 cupcakes

Ingredients
½ cup (1 stick) unsalted
  butter, softened
1¾ cups confectioners'
  sugar, sifted
a few drops of flavoring
  or food coloring (optional)

1 Put the butter in a large bowl. Beat in the confectioners' sugar a little at a time with a wooden spoon or electric whisk until smooth.

2 Stir in a few drops of flavoring or food coloring, if you like. Pipe or spread onto a large cake or cupcakes.

CREAM CHEESE FROSTING

Enough for an 8-inch cake or 12 cupcakes

Ingredients

¼ cup (½ stick) unsalted butter, softened
1¾ cups confectioners' sugar, sifted
¼ cup full-fat cream cheese
a few drops of flavoring or food coloring (optional)

1 Put the butter in a large bowl. Beat in the confectioners' sugar a little at a time with a wooden spoon or electric whisk until smooth.

2 Beat in half of the cream cheese. Add the rest of the cream cheese and beat until smooth.

3 Stir in a few drops of flavoring or food coloring, if you like. Pipe or spread onto a large cake or cupcakes.

First published 2021 by Button Books, an imprint of Guild of Master Craftsman Publications Ltd. Text © GMC Publications Ltd, 2021. Copyright in the Work @ GMC Publications Ltd, 2021. Illustrations © Esther Coombs, 2021. Recipes compiled by Laura Paton. ISBN 978 1 78708 109 3. Distributed by Publishers Group West in the United States. All rights reserved. The right of Esther Coombs © to be identified as the illustrator of this work has been asserted in accordance with the Copyright, Designs and Patents Act 1988, sections 77 and 78. No part of this publication may be reproduced, stored in a retrieval system, or transmitted in any form or by any means without the prior permission of the publisher and copyright owner. This book is sold subject to the condition that all designs are copyright and are not for commercial reproduction without the permission of the designer and copyright owner. The publishers and author can accept no legal responsibility for any consequences arising from the application of information, advice, or instructions given in this publication. A catalog record for this book is available from the British Library. Printed and bound in China.

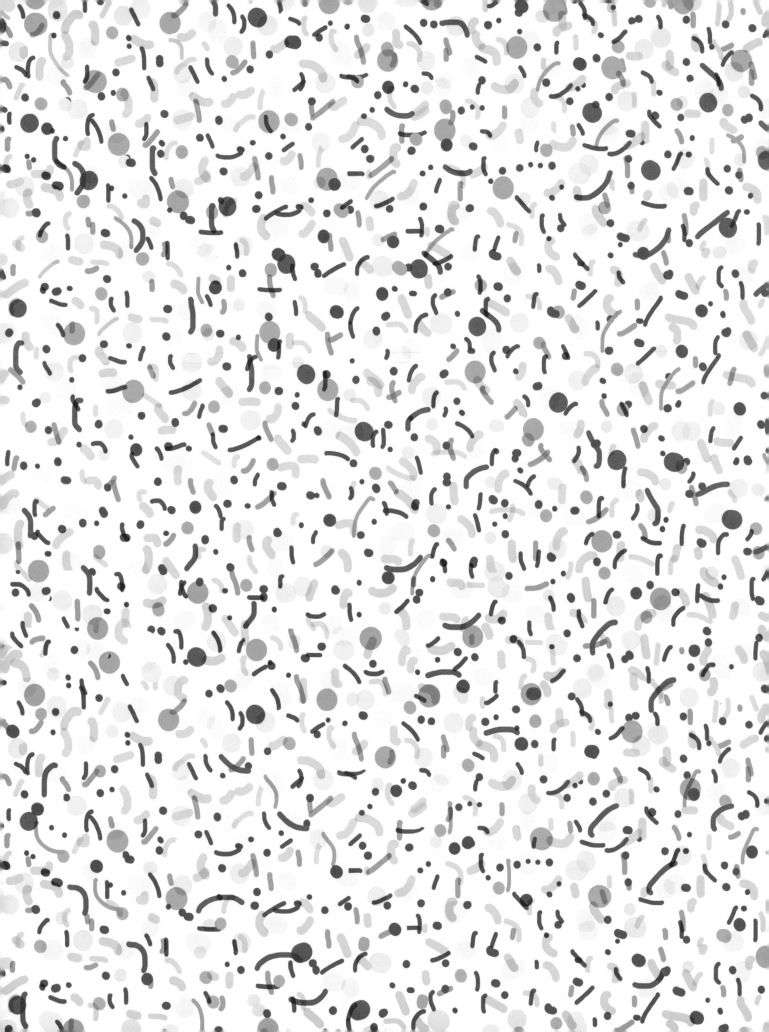